KEN DRYDEN

P9-BUH-301

FRED McFADDEN

SUPER PEOPLE

Fitzhenry and Whiteside

Ken Dryden
Fred McFadden

Copyright © 1976
Fitzhenry & Whiteside Limited
150 Lesmill Road
Don Mills, Ontario M3B 2T5

Editor   Diane Mew
Designer   Brant Cowie
Illustrator   David Simpson
Maps   Julian Cleva
Cartoon   M. R. Tingley, London Free Press
Photos   Denis Brodeur
            CP Picture Service
            Dryden Family
            Dennis Miles ,
            Dave Paterson
            Toronto Star

Superpeople Series
General Editor   Fred McFadden
Editor-in-Chief   Robert Read

No part of this publication may be
reproduced in any form or by any means
without permission in writing from the
publisher.

Printed and bound in Canada
ISBN 0-88902-325-5

CHAPTER 1

Canada vs Russia 1972

FINAL GAME TONIGHT

(Moscow – September 28, 1972) The final game of the Canada–Russia series will be played tonight. The series is now tied. Russia has won 3 games, Canada has won 3, one game was a tie. As the series goes down to the 8th game, Canadian fans are all asking one question — Can Canada come back to win the series?

Dryden against Yakushev

More than any other member of the team, Ken Dryden was nervous about the game. He had been picked by coach Harry Sinden to be the goalie. Ken had been in goal for the first game of the series in Montreal, which Canada had lost 7 – 3. He had also been the goalie in the fourth game in Vancouver when Russia had defeated Canada 5 – 3. Some of the sports writers and fans had suggested that Dryden had let in some easy goals. They said he had played two bad games in a row and that he was not in his top form. What was worse, Ken knew that he had not played well.

Now the eighth game was approaching. What if he was not up for the game? What if he let in a couple of soft goals? This was the most important game of his life. He knew that if other players made mistakes, they could be covered. But no one covered for the goalie, and there could be no excuses. His stomach felt strange; his legs were heavy and tired. And yet he looked forward to the opening face-off.

Game 8 – The Mos

Ken's nerves settled down as soon as the action began. He blocked one shot, and then caught a tough shot heading for the corner. As the play stopped, Phil Esposito skated by and said, "Way to go, big guy."

Millions of Canadians were watching the game on television. Since the game was being played in the evening, Moscow time, it was the afternoon in Canada. Many schools set up television sets for students to watch the game. They groaned as the Russians moved into the Canadian zone. They screamed with excitement as the Canadians rushed towards the Russian goal. However, by the end of the second period, the Russians were ahead 5 – 3.

In the dressing room of the Canadian team, the players were quiet. Ken Dryden was resting and thinking. There was no need for a rousing speech from the coach. All the players knew that there was only one period to go — only twenty

minutes left in which they had to score three goals to win. They knew that they would have to give everything they had, and then a little more, to pull out a win.

Two minutes into the third period, Phil Esposito scored. Then Yvan Cournoyer added the tying goal to make it 5 – 5. But there were still seven minutes left in the period. Ken played brilliantly to prevent the Russians from scoring. Finally, with just 34 seconds to go, Paul Henderson scored the winning goal. Ken Dryden, like all Canadians, was wild with excitement. He skated the length of the ice to join the triumphant group around Henderson.

In the midst of the celebration he suddenly stopped — there were still 34 seconds to go. These were the longest seconds of his life. At last, the horn blasted, and the game was over. Canada had won the game and the series by the narrowest of margins. Ken Dryden had risen to the challenge and played one of the greatest games of his life.

CHAPTER 2

The Early Years

Kenneth Wayne Dryden was born on August 8, 1947 in Hamilton, Ontario. He has one brother Dave, six years older, and a younger sister Judy. When Ken was very young, his family moved to Etobicoke, in suburban Toronto. It was here that Ken went to school and began to play sports.

Ken's father encouraged his boys to play hockey. He built a goalie net of wood and chicken wire for Dave, who was then nine years old. When Ken saw Dave playing goal with his friends, he wanted to copy his brother. Dave became an excellent goaltender and Ken was determined that he would be one too.

Their parents had a large area of the backyard paved, so that the boys could play hockey. Soon they had two goalie nets. Ken and Dave loved taking shots at each other, with a tennis ball or a puck. Who could score the most goals out of ten shots? Who could stop the most breakaways by the other? The boys practised goaltending in winter, fall and spring, and sometimes even in summer.

Dave in the home-made net

Ken Dryden played road hockey, or ball hockey, like most young Canadian boys. There were no sweaters, no jackets, no coaches and no referees. Yet it was always lots of fun. It was here that Ken and his brother learned how to catch the puck and how to play the angles against sharp-shooting opponents. These skills helped them to become professional goaltenders in later life.

My name is Kenneth
Wane Dryden.
I am seven years old
I live at 28 Pinehurst Cres
I go to Humber Valley
Village Public school.
My Phone numbe is
Mu 5574.
There are two children
in my family.
My hoby is Sports.

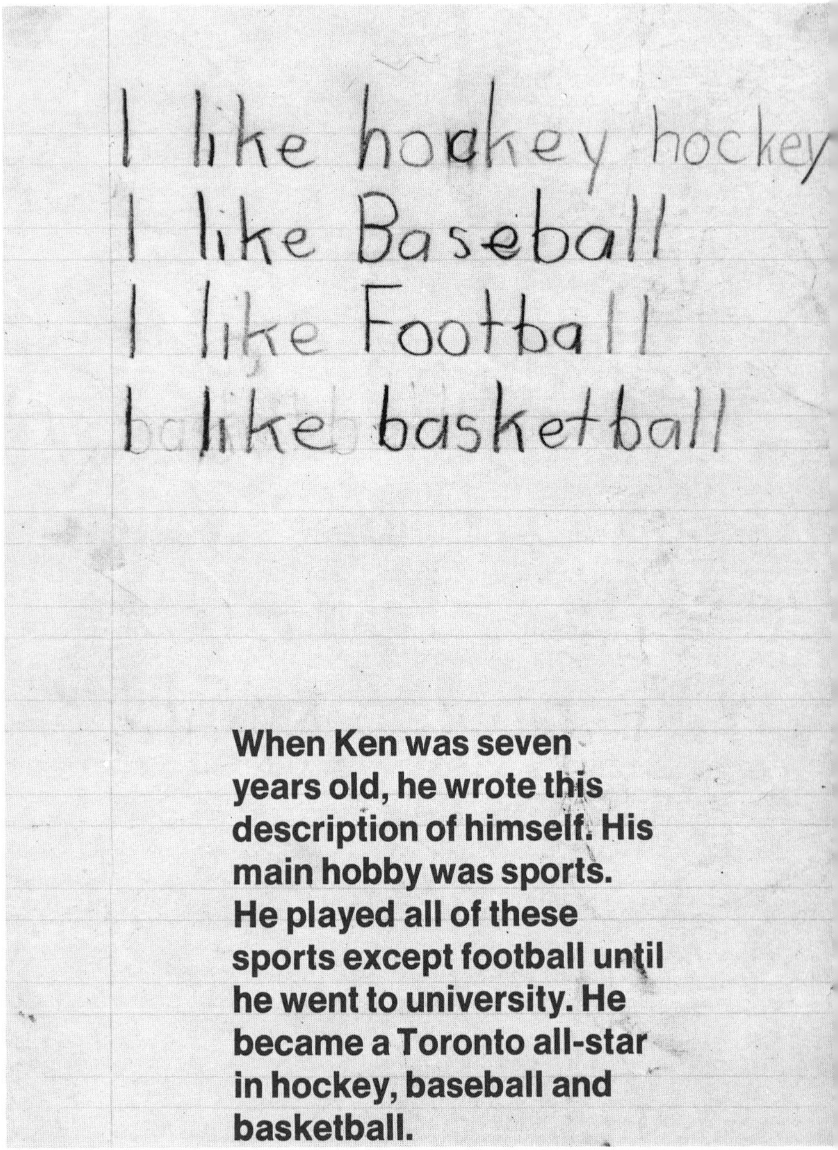

I like hockey hockey
I like Baseball
I like Football
ba like basketball

When Ken was seven years old, he wrote this description of himself. His main hobby was sports. He played all of these sports except football until he went to university. He became a Toronto all-star in hockey, baseball and basketball.

Ken at age 8

The Man From Mars

The Dryden boys played hockey after school and on most weekends. Since Ken was so small, his parents bought him a baseball catcher's mask and a football helmet, to protect him from injury. One day a friend saw young Ken in this outfit and said, "Look at the man from Mars."

Sometimes some of Dave's older friends didn't want to play hockey with his younger brother. Dave's reply was, "If you don't want Ken to play, then I don't want to play either." They always let young Ken play.

Ken admired several professional goalies, including Johnny Bower of the Toronto Maple Leafs. But his real hero was his older brother Dave. Whatever Dave could do, Ken would also try to do. This was one of the first challenges that Ken faced, and won.

Ken's parents believed that he would learn to play hockey better if he was in a league with older boys. So when Ken was seven, he started to play in a league against boys who were nine or ten. Ken soon became an excellent goalie.

Dave Dryden was also becoming a great netminder. He went on to play for the Chicago Black Hawks, Buffalo Sabres and the Edmonton Oilers. Dave was always an inspiration to Ken; the desire to be as good as his brother encouraged him to practise long hours, and to always give his best.

Ken played other sports as well. He was an all-star baseball pitcher with a great fast ball. He pitched many no-hit games. In addition, he was often the best hitter on the team. He was once given a tryout at a training camp run by the Baltimore Orioles. If he had not chosen a career in hockey, he might have become a pro baseball player.

**Top: Ken and Dave
in the net**

**Left: Ken and Dave
ready for baseball**

**Right: Ken and Judy in
Dave's equipment**

A Busy Boy

Ken was a good student and liked his schoolwork. He enjoyed reading, especially about sports, and he kept a scrapbook of newspaper reports of important sports events and other news.

When he was ten, he needed some extra money. He asked his parents if they would pay him for picking the large crop of dandelions on their lawn. His father said that they would pay him 2¢ for each dandelion picked, if he did a good job and pulled up the roots as well.

Ken started picking dandelions. A few days later, he showed his parents several bushel baskets full of dandelions. When the dandelions were counted they were worth $81.68. Ken used the money to buy what he had set his heart on: a globe and a set of encyclopedia.

In this way, Ken learned the value of money. And even now, though he earns a large salary, he still watches his money carefully and spends it wisely.

Dave, Judy and Ken

When Ken was eleven, he started missing long shots on goal. He had his eyes tested, and it was found that he was short sighted. But that didn't stop him. He was fitted with contact lenses for playing hockey. He still wears contacts while playing goal in the NHL.

Mr. and Mrs. Dryden say, "We encouraged Judy and the boys to play sports. But we always told them that school was just as important. We wanted the two things to go together. Both Ken and Dave have always felt that their education is as important as their sports career."

When Ken went to high school, he was always busy. He became a city all-star in both basketball and hockey. Because the two seasons ran at the same time, he had to organize his time carefully. He usually came home at 3:30 and did his homework before supper. In the evening, he played basketball or hockey.

Ken jumps for the Etobicoke Rams

CHAPTER 3

The Big Decision

By the time Ken had completed his fourth year at
Etobicoke Collegiate, he had been noticed by
hockey scouts. He was drafted by the Montreal
Canadiens, and given a chance to play for their
Junior A team in Peterborough. However, Ken
knew that it would be difficult to complete his final
year of high school if he were not living at home.
So he chose to stay at home and complete his year.
He played for Etobicoke in the Junior B league, and
was picked as the all-star goalie.

When Ken completed high school, he had
several choices. He could have played Junior A
hockey in Ontario. This was the usual path for
hockey players hoping to play in the NHL. He
received offers of scholarships from many American universities. He had a very tempting offer from
the University of Minnesota, one of the leading
hockey schools in the United States. Their hockey
scholarship would have been worth $10,000 over
the four years at university, for his room and board
and other expenses.

Cornell

However, Ken was not only interested in playing hockey; he wanted a good education as well. He finally decided to attend Cornell University, in Ithaca, New York. Cornell was not famous as a hockey school, but it had an excellent educational record. All he received there was a scholarship award worth $200 a year. He worked as a waiter and dishwasher to help pay his way through college.

Ken went to Cornell for four years. While he was there, Cornell had one of the top college hockey teams in the United States. Many people said that this was largely due to Ken. He was the winning goalie in 67 games, and lost only 3. He is probably the best goalie to have ever played in college hockey in the United States, and was selected to the All-American team three times. In 1969, he was named as the outstanding athlete at Cornell. When he graduated from the university in 1970, the Montreal Canadiens had a professional contract waiting for him.

While at Cornell, Ken met a pretty girl named Lynda. On their first date they went swimming. At that time, Lynda didn't even know that Ken was a great hockey player.

"He was one of the shyest boys I ever met. Even after we were going out together, he was very quiet and modest."

But Lynda continued to date Ken through the Cornell years, and they were married in 1970.

The Voyageurs

After college, Ken was faced with another big decision. He had decided that he wanted to be a lawyer. If he turned pro with the Canadiens he would have to give up his career as a lawyer, and if he went to law school, he would have to give up playing in a good hockey league. How could he study to be a lawyer, without giving up the excitement and thrills of playing goal?

He decided to accept an offer to play for the Canadian National team in Winnipeg, Manitoba in 1969-70. This was a group of excellent amateur hockey players, who had been gathered together to play for Canada against teams from other countries in tournaments in Canada and Europe.

Unfortunately, the Canadian team folded in 1970. Ken decided to go to McGill Law School, in

Montreal, and to try out as goalie for the Montreal Canadiens' farm team, the Voyageurs.

When Ken went to the Montreal training camp, it was his first chance to play against the pros. He wondered, "How will I do against players like Jean Beliveau, Peter Mahovlich, Henri Richard or Yvan Cournoyer?"

Ken played well in training camp. He satisfied himself that he could play against the pros. But Montreal already had Rogatien Vachon and Phil Myre as regular goaltenders. Ken was assigned to be a part-time goalie of the Voyageurs, while continuing as a full-time student at McGill.

As the 1970-71 season progressed, Ken played more games with the Voyageurs and became the first-string goalie. He soon became the best goalie in the American League. Sam Pollock, the Montreal general manager, watched Ken carefully. The Canadiens were not completely happy with their regular goalies. Towards the end of the 1971 season, they brought Ken up to the big team — the Montreal Canadiens.

It was one thing to excel at Cornell or with the Voyageurs. Now Ken would have to face the superstars of the NHL. He thought, "Will I be able to stop Phil Esposito, or Bobby Hull, or Bobby Orr?"

CHAPTER 4

The Rookie Faces the Pros

Ken's first NHL game was in Pittsburgh. He was glad that it was not in Montreal. The pressure of playing before the home fans would be tremendous. Playing in Pittsburgh would be an easier start.

"My legs were like jelly before the first game. My knees were shaking so hard, I thought that everybody in the place would notice it. Usually my nerves settle down when the game begins, but I was nervous all through that first game."

Ken's nerves did not stop him from playing a very good game, and the Canadiens won 5 – 1.

A few days later against the New York Rangers, Ken played a fantastic game. He stopped 47 shots and Canadiens won 6 – 2. Ken played in six games at the end of the season, and Montreal won every game.

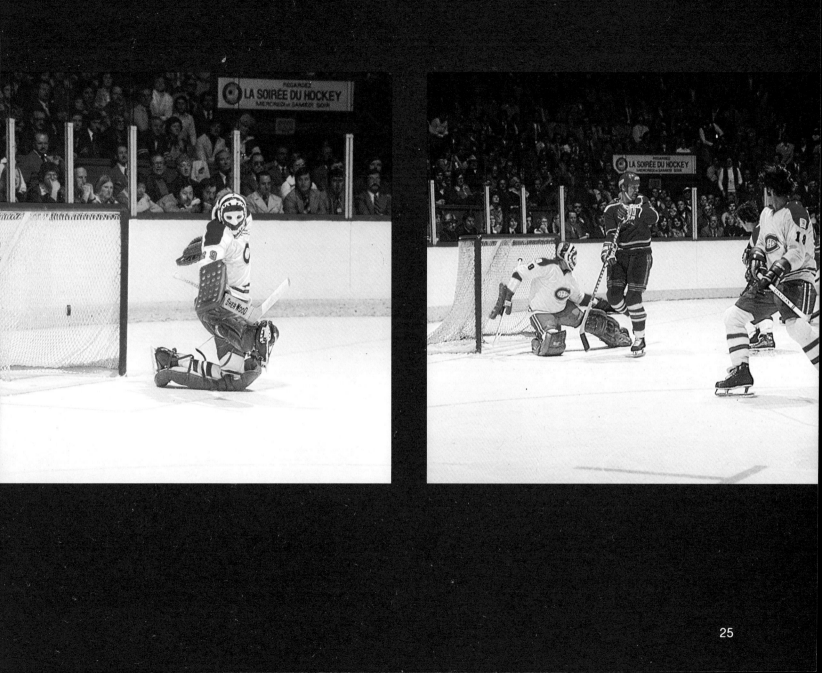

Now the Canadiens entered the Stanley Cup playoffs. First they faced the big, bad Bruins from Boston, with Phil Esposito and Bobby Orr. Would the coach go with one of his regular reliable goalies, or would he gamble with his spectacular rookie? Coach Al McNeil played a hunch and started young Ken Dryden.

In the series against Boston, Dryden was superb. He played the angles on the long shots beautifully; he sprawled to protect the net when the Bruins were in close. For a big man, he moved very quickly, and his left hand flashed out to catch shots that looked like sure goals. Canadiens upset the favoured Bruins and won the series 4 games to 3. Boston's Phil Esposito said, "If there's one man who beat us, it was Ken Dryden."

Ken Dryden has mixed feelings about giving autographs. He thinks that an autograph should be something personal between two people. This is difficult when you are signing autographs in a big crowd. However, he remembers when he was a young boy, he collected autographs.

"I remember getting Frank Mahovlich's autograph at a hockey banquet. I was very thrilled. I know how much it means to young kids, so I will continue to give autographs."

Montreal won the next series against Minnesota, 4 games to 2. The finals were against Chicago Black Hawks, led by the great Bobby Hull and Stan Mikita. Each team won its home games, and the series was tied three games each. The last game was in Chicago, giving them the home rink advantage.

In the final game Chicago jumped into a 2-goal lead. They continued to pour shots on the Montreal goal, but Dryden blocked them all. By the third period, Canadiens had tied it up. Finally Henri Richard scored the winner and Montreal were now the Stanley Cup champions.

Throughout all 20 games of the Stanley Cup series, the young rookie had been outstanding. He was selected as the winner of the Conn Smythe trophy as the best player in the Stanley Cup playoffs.

The First Full Season In The NHL

The 1971-72 season was Ken's first full year in the NHL. Many wondered if he could keep up his excellent play as goalie.

"Dryden just had a lucky streak," some fans scoffed. "He'll never last a full season."

They were wrong. In the face of this challenge Ken proved that he could play well all year. He won the Calder trophy as the best rookie in the NHL, and he was selected for the second All-Star team. In 1972-73 he was selected for the first All-Star team and also won the Vezina trophy as the top goalie in the league.

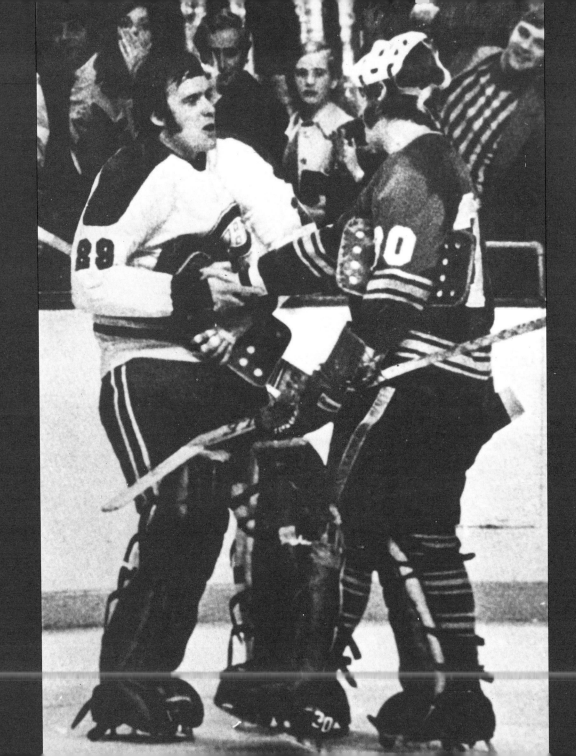

Ken is now regarded as one of the best net-minders in the history of the NHL. He is regarded as one of the nicest guys as well. In spite of his successes, he is still a very quiet and modest person.

He has never been in a fight in a hockey game. He believes that you show your courage in ways other than fighting. In one game, John McKenzie skated into his crease, and Ken accidentally clipped him on the nose with his stick.

"Excuse me," said Ken.

"I was ready for war," said McKenzie, "but how do you get mad at a nice guy like that?"

Ken does not hold with the win-at-all-cost idea. "I don't believe that winning is everything and losing is a disgrace. But you have to want to win very much. If you're going to be a good goalie, you have to hate the thought of letting the puck go past you. You have to be prepared to do anything within the rules to win. But if you have done your best and lose, there is no need to be ashamed about it."

Ken has always believed that the real winner in sports, and in life, is the person who plays by the rules, and does his very best.

Ken and Dave are the only brothers to have faced each other as goalies in the history of the NHL. Here Ken greets Dave at centre ice after a game with the Buffalo Sabres.

A New Team-Nader's Raiders

In the summer of 1971, Ken worked for Ralph Nader, an American lawyer who is the leader of a group called "Nader's Raiders." They provide information and press governments to take action about problems such as water and air pollution, and automobile safety. Ken worked without a regular salary for the summer. He was paid $400, but he turned it back to Ralph Nader to help in his work.

"It was a worthwhile summer for me. I gained a lot of good experience. Besides, the Nader group could use the money in a more useful manner than I could."

As a result of that summer's work, Ken is now interested in working to protect our air and water — to preserve a healthy environment. He also wants to help consumers — the people who buy goods from stores and factories. He feels that some manufacturers do not give people full value for their money.

When Ken retires from hockey, he will probably continue this work of helping to protect other people. He feels that is more important than just earning a lot of money.

CHAPTER 5

Some New Challenges

During the 1960's, Canadian amateur hockey teams played against other teams in Europe in world championships. Up until this time, Canadian teams had won most games. During the 1960's, however, the Russians won almost every series. In spite of these defeats, most Canadians were confident that a team of Canadian professional players from the NHL would easily beat a Russian team.

The first Canada – Russia series was announced in 1972. Coach Harry Sinden of the Boston Bruins collected the best team of professionals available, including such stars as Phil Esposito, Frank and Peter Mahovlich, Bobby Clarke and Brad Park. For goal, he picked Tony Esposito, and Ken Dryden.

Ken was not quite as certain about beating the Russians as some of the sports writers and players. He had great respect for their skating and passing. He knew that they would be in better

physical condition than the Canadians. Yet he believed that Canada would win the series. He really looked forward to the excitement of meeting the Russians.

Boris Mikhailov tips a goal past Dryden and Bill White

Valary Kharlamov scores on Dryden

During his first two games in Canada, Ken did not play well. He had let in 12 goals and he was tremendously depressed at his poor performance.

"Maybe I just can't play against the Russians," he thought. He knew his goaltending had not been as good as Tony Esposito's, who had let in only 5 goals in the other two games in Canada. Still, he hoped for one more chance. This was a personal challenge that he wanted to overcome.

Canada lost the first game in Moscow, by a score of 5 – 4, and coach Sinden selected Ken to play in game 6. Canada won this game 3 – 2, and Dryden was a star. He had changed his style to suit the quick, short passes by the Russians, and it had worked.

In game 8, when Canada won the series, Ken Dryden played magnificently. He had overcome his own fear of failure. It was the high point of his career.

"The Canada – Russia series meant more to me than all of the other things that I have achieved in hockey."

Ken and Lynda in Moscow in 1972

Ken the law student

A Surprising Choice

Just before the beginning of the 1973 season, Ken Dryden stunned the sports world by announcing that he was retiring for one year, to work in a lawyer's office in Toronto. This year of apprenticeship was necessary if he was going to practise law. His hockey salary would have been about $80,000 for one season; his salary as a law student was $7,000.

Some people could not believe that he would turn down so much money. They said to him, "You must be crazy!"

Ken thought to himself, "Maybe I am, but I think I'm right." He had decided to complete his preparations for being a lawyer, and was prepared to take his chances when he returned to hockey.

During his year away from the Montreal Canadiens, he maintained contact with hockey. Like most goalies, Ken Dryden dreamed about playing another position. So during the year off, he played in an amateur league as a defenceman. Some of the big league scouts watched him. They all agreed that he would never be another Bobby Orr.

Return To The NHL

Ken returned to the NHL for the 1974-75 season. He saw this return as another challenge. Could he continue as a top goalie after a year's layoff? He was determined to report to training camp in good physical condition. He ran every day, and played tennis and squash regularly. He watched his diet carefully. When training camp began, he was well below his last year's playing weight.

When the season began, he was a little rusty. But by Christmas he was as good as ever. Today he continues to be a superstar.

How good is Ken Dryden? Ken feels that he does not have special ability. "I have a certain amount of natural ability in hockey and other things. But I work hard at it. Anything worthwhile requires extra effort." When he saw himself playing on a television replay, he was disappointed.

"I thought that I was as graceful as a ballet dancer, but I wasn't. In fact, I flopped around, and looked quite awkward."

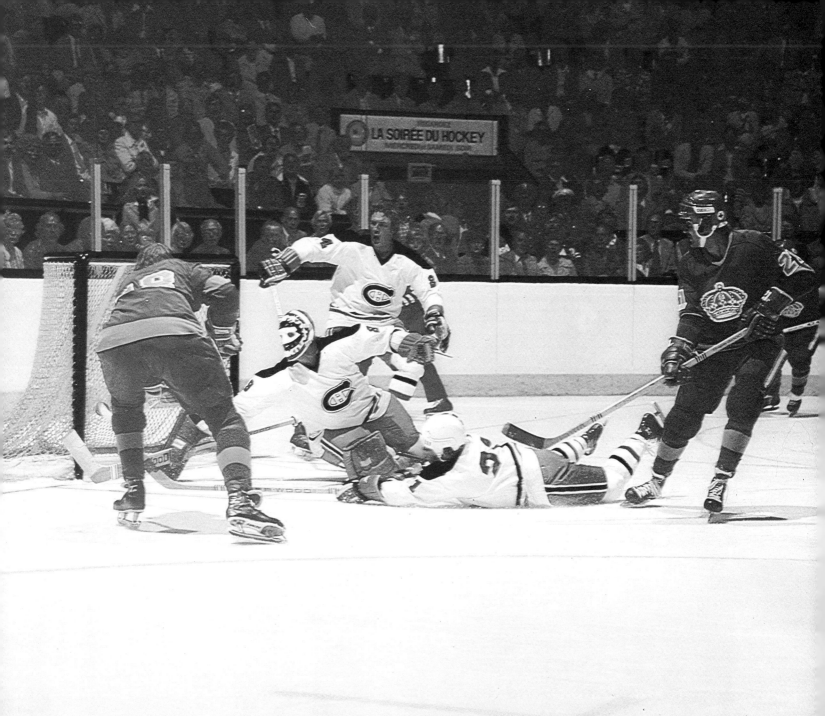

Ken is a big man. He is 193 cm (6'4") high, and weighs 93 kg (205 pounds). He is a smart goalie, and moves carefully to cut off the shooter's angle. A great asset is his ability to catch shots.

"He has the best catching hand of any goalie in the NHL," says Phil Esposito.

King Clancy of the Maple Leafs has seen goalies in pro hockey for 50 years. King says, "He's as good as any goalkeeper I've ever seen."

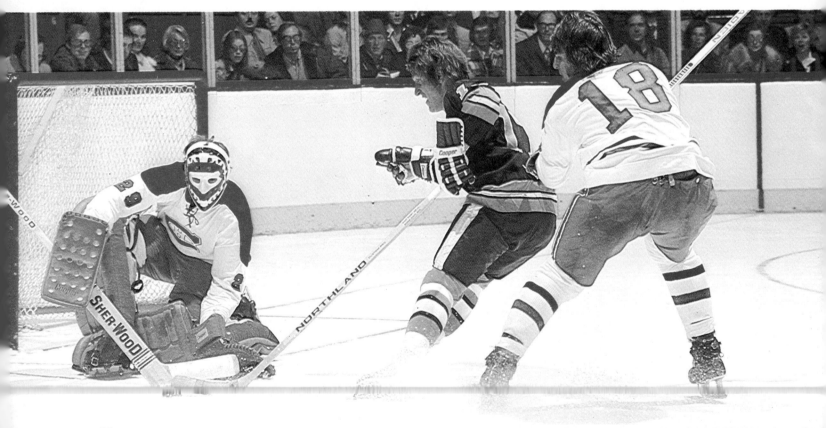

A Canadian Hero

Ken Dryden has faced many challenges in his life. As a boy, he wanted to imitate his older brother Dave. As a teenager, he wanted to excel in sports. As a student, he wanted to keep up good school grades. In all these challenges he has been successful.

Some hockey officials told him that the only way to make the NHL was to play junior hockey in Ontario. He chose instead to go to Cornell and get a good education while playing hockey. He helped Montreal to a Stanley Cup championship, even though some said that he was just a good college goalie. He faced his greatest personal challenge by helping to defeat the Russians in 1972. He has become an all-star goalie in the NHL. Still he has maintained his varied interests outside of hockey, and has shown his concern for helping others.

"I have never worried about the future. I think that you can only prepare for the future so far. You have to be prepared for changes, and try to handle each one as it comes up."

No one can be sure what the future holds for Ken Dryden. It is likely that he will continue for some years to be an excellent goalie in professional hockey. It is probable that he will continue to be concerned about helping people. One thing is certain — he will continue to make his decisions by doing what he thinks is right.

45

QUEBEC
Montreal

ONTARIO
Peterborough
Toronto
Etobicoke
Hamilton

Winnipeg
MANITOBA

Boston
MASSACHUSETTS

Ithaca
NEW YORK
Buffalo

New York

Minneapolis
MINNESOTA

Baltimore
MARYLAND

Chicago
ILLINOIS

Pittsburgh
PENNSYLVANIA

La Soirée du Hockey

SUPER PEOPLE   **Ken Dryden**